LIFE IN THE ROMAN EMPIRE

PATRICIANS IN THE ROMAN EMPIRE

DENISE JACOBS

Cavendish
Square

New York

Published in 2017 by Cavendish Square Publishing, LLC
243 5th Avenue, Suite 136, New York, NY 10016

Copyright © 2017 by Cavendish Square Publishing, LLC

First Edition

Website: cavendishsq.com

This publication represents the opinions and views of the author based on his or her personal experience, knowledge, and research. The information in this book serves as a general guide only. The author and publisher have used their best efforts in preparing this book and disclaim liability rising directly or indirectly from the use and application of this book.

CPSIA Compliance Information: Batch #CW17CSQ

All websites were available and accurate when this book was sent to press.

Library of Congress Cataloging-in-Publication Data

Names: Jacobs, Denise, author.
Title: Patricians in the Roman Empire / Denise Jacobs.
Description: New York : Cavendish Square Publishing, [2017] | Series: Life in the Roman Empire | Includes bibliographical references and index.
Identifiers: LCCN 2016021849 (print) | LCCN 2016031731 (ebook) | ISBN 9781502622570 (library bound) | ISBN 9781502622587 (E-book)
Subjects: LCSH: Patricians (Rome)--History--Juvenile literature. | Social classes--Rome--History--Juvenile literature. | Rome--Social conditions--Juvenile literature. | Rome--Social life and customs--Juvenile literature. | Rome--History--Empire, 30 B.C.-476 A.D.--Juvenile literature.
Classification: LCC DG83.3 .J33 2017 (print) | LCC DG83.3 (ebook) | DDC 305.5/20937--dc23
LC record available at https://lccn.loc.gov/2016021849

Editorial Director: David McNamara
Editor: Caitlyn Miller
Copy Editor: Nathan Heidelberger
Assistant Art Director: Amy Greenan
Designer: Joseph Macri
Production Assistant: Karol Szymczuk
Photo Research: J8 Media

Printed in the United States of America

Contents

WHO RULED THE ROMAN EMPIRE?

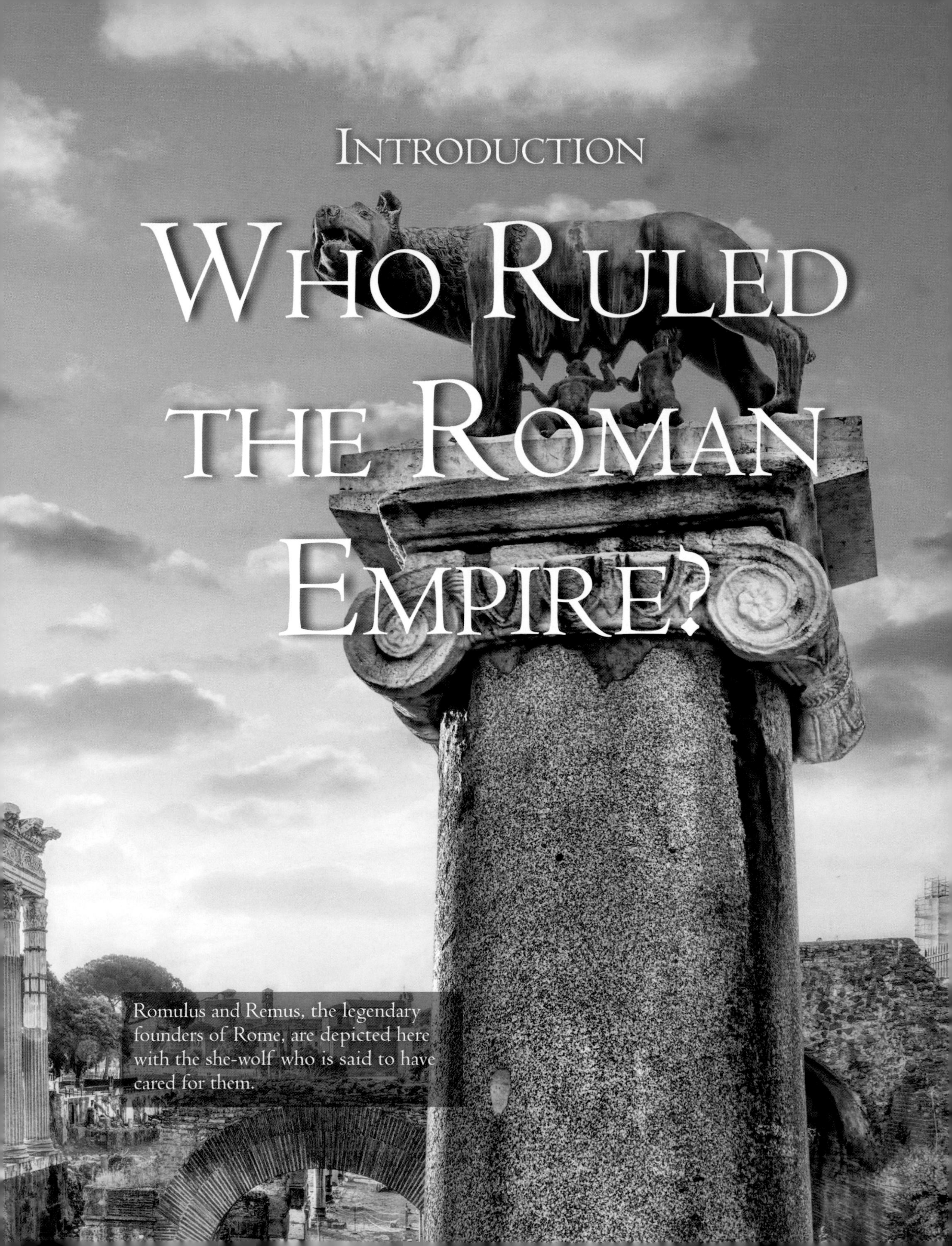

Romulus and Remus, the legendary founders of Rome, are depicted here with the she-wolf who is said to have cared for them.

Today we associate ancient Rome with togas, **gladiators**, and emperors. When we think of the empire, the larger-than-life figures who ruled spring to mind. Who doesn't know of Julius Caesar's power (and his downfall)? Yet there is so much more to ancient Rome than chariot races and marble statues.

According to the Romans themselves, their city was founded in 753 BCE. Even the beginnings of the empire are steeped in myth. The ancient Romans recounted the legend of Romulus and Remus, whom they believed to be the founders of Rome. The twins were the sons of a mortal woman and the god of war, Mars. Their story is one of violence and intrigue. It ends with Romulus killing his brother and naming the city of Rome after himself.

Much like the myth of the city's foundation, the history of the empire is filled with violent conquest and sometimes brutal displays of power. Under Augustus's rule, Rome controlled all of Italy and the rest of mainland Europe west of the Rhine River and south of the Danube River, as well as much of North Africa and the Middle East.

In fact, at its height, the Roman Empire reached all the way from Britain to Persia. It brought together an array of European, African, and Middle Eastern peoples, forming a vibrant multicultural society. In spite of a spirit of tolerance and understanding, a rigid social structure solidified in ancient Rome.

At the top of the hierarchy stood the emperor, followed by a group of citizens from powerful families. The members of this ruling class were known as **patricians**. In this book you will meet emperors, senators, generals, and poets, as well as women and children of the imperial court. Step back in time and imagine what it might have been like to live among Rome's patricians when Rome was at its most powerful, from 27 BCE to around 200 CE. Picture lavish lifestyles and daring power plays. Think of banquets and fragile politics. This was life as a patrician in the Roman Empire.

CHAPTER ONE

EMPERORS AND THE SENATE

Fabius the Delayer served as consul five times.

In 509 BCE, ancient Rome transitioned from a kingdom to a republic. This transition was marked by the removal of the last of seven kings, Tarquin the Proud, from the throne. Ancient Romans resented the last few kings in the line—they saw these rulers as corrupt tyrants. The Roman Republic aimed to avoid the problem of absolute power. Instead of a single leader, two **consuls** presided. Each consul was elected and faced reelection each year. These two men shared **imperium**, the authority to command troops and to interpret and carry out the law. Consuls and other government officials were chosen by assemblies that were open to all male Roman citizens—that is, free men who met certain other qualifications.

The consuls led the Senate, which created laws, oversaw spending, and negotiated foreign relations. Unlike the consuls, members of the Senate were not elected. They were appointed, and these appointments lasted for life. Yet the republic ended in 31 BCE when an empire took its place. When we think of ancient Rome's government, the empire is often what comes to mind.

From Republic to Empire

Rome's republican government was not "of the people, by the people, and for the people" in the sense that we understand today. Only wealthy nobles—a small portion of the population—were in a position to take active part in government and politics. These people cherished their freedom from one-man rule. However, as Rome conquered more and more of the Mediterranean world, the republic became increasingly difficult to govern efficiently. And as Rome grew more powerful and wealthy, there were Roman politicians and generals who could not resist the temptation to acquire some of that wealth and power for themselves.

In 44 BCE, Julius Caesar, the victor in a brutal civil war that had threatened to destroy the republic, had himself declared dictator for life. In the past, the consuls sometimes appointed a dictator to take absolute command of the army and government during an emergency—but the dictator's term only lasted six months. Caesar's move angered many senators, and a group of them murdered him—but they could not save the republic. After another fourteen years of civil war, Caesar's grandnephew and adopted son Octavian emerged victorious. In 27 BCE, the Senate gave him the title Augustus (meaning "revered" or "worthy of honor"), and he claimed that he had restored the republic. In reality, he alone now controlled Rome—and its empire.

Concentration of Power

Augustus, an extremely intelligent and diplomatic man, was careful not to make the mistake that had doomed Julius Caesar. Instead of proclaiming himself dictator or king, he took the title **princeps**, "first citizen." Operating within the framework that had upheld Rome for nearly five hundred years, he served as one of the two annually elected consuls.

The old republican forms of government were carefully maintained. The Senate and assemblies still met, and the powers that Augustus wielded were clearly defined, not arbitrary.

Augustus was Rome's first emperor.

The princeps, however, was so enormously wealthy and influential that over the course of many years he was able to acquire the powers of every important office in the Roman government. For nine years in a row, Augustus was elected a consul. After this, he was given lifelong tribunician power—the power that, in the republic, had belonged to officials called tribunes—enabling him to veto any laws, elections, decrees of the Senate, or actions of other officials. The Senate also repeatedly voted Augustus control of the provinces of Egypt, Gaul (present-day France and Belgium), Spain, and Syria—the large, important provinces where most of Rome's military forces were stationed. In 12 BCE, he was even elected to the lifelong position of high priest of the Roman state religion. It is no wonder that, as the historian Dio Cassius wrote around 200 CE, "Nothing … was done which did not please Augustus."

Some senators resented the new state of affairs. Most Romans, however, seemed glad to accept the rule of Augustus. People were tired of decades of civil war and were grateful to the princeps for bringing peace and prosperity back to Rome. They felt that the government was now far more stable and efficient, and much less corrupt, than it had been in the later years of the republic. Augustus further won the people's favor by such actions as beautifying the city of Rome, renovating its temples, improving its water supply, sponsoring free public entertainment, and lowering the price of grain. He gave land or money to all retiring soldiers and several times distributed money from his personal funds, or grain bought with his own money, to hundreds of thousands of Roman commoners.

THE LEGACY OF AUGUSTUS

Even on his deathbed, Augustus was aware of all he had done to strengthen the empire. Augustus felt that under his leadership, Rome had become an untouchable superpower. The final statement he made reflected this feeling. According to historians, his last words directed to the public were, "I found Rome of clay; I leave it to you of marble." The Roman Senate declared Augustus a god following his death, and his cremated remains were interred in an opulent tomb.

Augustus ruled the Roman Empire for some forty years, dying in 14 CE at the age of about seventy-six. He had made sure that his stepson Tiberius would succeed him as princeps: during Augustus's lifetime, the Senate had given Tiberius tribunician power and imperium, and he had successfully served in a number of military and administrative posts. As the heir of Augustus's wealth and a man experienced in public service, Tiberius was easily accepted as emperor. Strabo, a Greek historian writing during the reign of Tiberius, affirmed that "the Romans and their allies have never enjoyed such an abundance of peace and prosperity as that which Augustus Caesar provided from the time when he first assumed absolute power, and which his son and successor, Tiberius, is now providing."

By Tiberius's death in 37 CE, it was clear that one-man rule was in Rome to stay. It had taken Augustus decades to accumulate his powers, and Tiberius had also gradually acquired his authority during years of training and government service. But Tiberius's successor, his great-nephew Gaius Caligula, became princeps without having held any office. Nevertheless, the Senate voted to give him all the powers that had been held by Augustus and Tiberius, and so it was with the emperors who followed. The Senate and people of Rome had come to accept without question the emperors' power, in the words of Dio Cassius, "to make levies, to collect money, to declare war, to make peace, to rule foreigners and citizens alike, anytime, anywhere."

POLITICS AND THE SENATE

During Rome's centuries as a republic, the Senate had been supreme. Senators and their families made up the wealthiest and most privileged class in Roman society. Even as Augustus accumulated his powers of government, he was careful to maintain the best possible relationship with the Senate, since it represented the interests of the wealthy and influential nobility. The highest government posts were still reserved for the senators. The Senate and its members also continued to deal with routine government business in Italy and in the provinces that were not under the emperor's direct control.

Augustus and Tiberius both made important changes in the Senate's activities and procedures. Augustus tried to make the Senate a more efficient body by decreasing its size from a thousand men to about six hundred. He also gave it a new role as a high court of law, hearing and judging cases of political importance (although some later emperors preferred to judge such cases themselves). In 5 BCE, Augustus set another pattern for the future by having two pairs of consuls elected every year, each pair serving a six-month term. Soon after coming to power, Tiberius did away with elections in the assemblies, which afterward met only for ceremonial purposes. From that time, all officials were elected by the Senate, and laws were passed by decrees of the Senate or edicts from the emperor.

The relationship between emperors and the Senate varied depending on circumstances and the people involved. Some emperors worked well with the Senate, while others—who were felt to seriously abuse their power—were hated by the Senate. Few senators could take the chance of standing up to the all-powerful emperor. At the same time, most emperors felt that it was wise not to offend the Senate, for they depended on senators to carry out many government functions. In any case, it soon became standard for senators to be nominated for office by the emperor himself. This meant that the Senate was largely filled with men loyal to the emperor (although they might not be so loyal to a succeeding emperor). The consuls and other officials had more prestige than real power. As the great Roman historian Tacitus put it, the senators had accepted the "futility of long speeches in the Senate, when the best men were quick to reach agreement elsewhere, and of endless haranguing of public meetings, when the final decisions were taken not by the ignorant multitude but by one man."

The Commander in Chief

Much of the emperor's power came from his control of the army. Early on, Augustus had taken an additional first name, Imperator—the source of our word "emperor"—meaning "commander in chief." (During the republic, this had been a title granted to generals only temporarily, in honor of great victories.) By the seventies CE, Imperator had become the usual title of the Roman ruler, highlighting his role as supreme military commander.

The imperial Roman army was made up of twenty-five to thirty-three units called legions, with around five thousand men in each. The legions were generally stationed along the empire's borders or in provinces where trouble was likely to arise. Auxiliaries—additional troops made up mostly of non–Roman citizens—supported the legions. Each legion was commanded by a legionary **legate**, a senator appointed by the emperor. A provincial governor—also chosen by the emperor—had military authority over all the legions stationed in his province. When there was fighting to be done in a province, it was generally the governor who took charge of the campaign as the emperor's representative.

A number of emperors led the army themselves. The emperor Trajan, for instance, waged three wars during his reign, adding to the empire Armenia, Mesopotamia, and Dacia, a large territory north of the Danube. Trajan was extremely popular with the army because he shared their dangers and hardships on campaign—and he seems to have genuinely enjoyed military life. Dio Cassius wrote, "Even if he did delight in war, nevertheless he was satisfied when success had been achieved, a most bitter foe overthrown and his countrymen exalted."

Sometimes when an emperor died and it was unclear who should succeed him, the army would declare one of its generals the new emperor. The army

Trajan became emperor because of his military prowess; he constructed this bridge between 102 and 106 CE as a testament to his power.

Patricians in the Roman Empire

might even oust an emperor to replace him with its own candidate. During the year 69 CE, this happened more than once. First the legions stationed in Germany revolted against the emperor Galba and proclaimed their commander, Vitellius, emperor. Galba was assassinated shortly afterward, and soldiers in the city of Rome declared another man emperor, Otho.

A brief civil war ended in the death of Otho, but Vitellius's rule was not secure. The legions in Egypt and along the Danube River supported a new claimant to the throne, Vespasian, a popular general with an impressive service record. By the end of 69, Vespasian's forces were in control of Rome. Vespasian proved himself worthy of the army's faith in him, ruling the empire justly and wisely for ten years. The events of the year 69, however, proved an important point. Just as emperors controlled the Senate but also needed its support, so it was with the army: an emperor who did not have the army behind him was unlikely to stay in power for long.

Power at the Top

Rome's development—from a kingdom to a republic to an empire—occurred because of those at the top of the social hierarchy. The patricians were the pool from which emperors and senators were chosen. The emperor and the Senate wielded a kind of power that many Romans would never grasp. And this power manifested as military might. As we'll see in the next chapter, power also manifested as personal wealth.

Chapter Two

Demonstrations of Wealth and Power

This temple in modern-day France is known as the Maison Carrée; it was built by Augustus.

"I built the senate-house and the Chalcidicum which adjoins
it and the temple of Apollo on the Palatine with porticos,
the temple of divine Julius, the Lupercal, the portico at the
Flaminian circus …"
—Augustus

Most emperors demonstrated their wealth and power in the form of new (and imposing) structures. Sometimes emperors' construction programs were for the people: Augustus alone restored eighty-two temples in one year. Other emperors, along with family members and the court, funded everything from government buildings to bathhouses and theaters, along with bridges, **aqueducts**, and roads. It was not just Rome that benefitted from the emperors' construction programs—the rest of Italy, and the provinces, too, received aqueducts, roads, and buildings and monuments of many kinds. However, many of the most impressive building projects were for the benefit of the emperor himself. Emperors were known to live in custom-built, luxurious homes.

LAVISH ESTATES

Augustus preferred to live fairly simply, or at least no more opulently than other upper-class Romans. Since he did not want to be seen as a king, he did not live in a palace but in a regular house. It was not especially elegant—marble was used nowhere in the house, nor were there any mosaic floors. There were, however, wall paintings, which were common in all upper-class Roman homes. And at his summer house on the island of Capri, he displayed his collections of fossils and ancient weapons.

Few of the emperors who came after Augustus shared his simple tastes. Tiberius built an imperial residence on Rome's Palatine Hill; it is from Palatine that we get the word "palace." Many later emperors lived in the palace built for Domitian on top of the Palatine (completed in 92 CE). Everything about Domitian's palace was designed to impress people with the emperor's might. The walls of the entryway were 98 feet (30 meters) high; the audience hall, or throne room, was gigantic; and the dining room used for state banquets was almost as large. These rooms were decorated with huge statues, rich wall paintings, and marble (in thin sheets on both walls and floors) in a wide range of colors, imported from all over the empire. The private apartments, where the imperial family lived, were just as splendid. Domitian's palace also featured a curved, two-story covered walkway along the south side of the building; four courtyards (one with a fountain surrounded by an octagonal maze); and a huge sunken garden in the shape of a racetrack.

Nearly every emperor also had several residences outside the city of Rome—**villas** in the countryside, summer houses by the sea. The most famous and elaborate of all these retreats was the emperor Hadrian's villa in Tivoli, about 15 miles (24 kilometers) east of Rome. Hadrian, who ruled from 117 to 138, was an amateur architect and designed much of the villa himself. It took

The ruins of Domitian's palace

ten years to construct the buildings and landscape the grounds. When the complex was finished, it was nearly one-tenth the size of the city of Rome.

Along with a palace, the estate included temples, bathhouses, guesthouses, banquet halls, two libraries, a theater, a swimming pool, an art gallery, and acres and acres of gardens. There were quarters for numerous servants and guards, underground service passages, and kitchens where food could be prepared for hundreds of people at once. The crown jewel of Tivoli was the emperor's personal retreat, an elegant house on a small island surrounded by a canal, which was in turn encircled by columns and statues; the whole retreat was enclosed by a high circular wall. The only way to the island was across a single bridge, which the emperor could even remove when he especially wanted to be left alone.

Public Works

Hadrian, like most emperors, did not build just for his own pleasure. He traveled throughout the empire, visiting thirty-eight of the empire's forty-four provinces. The *Augustan Histories* tell us that "in almost every city he constructed some building." In Rome itself, Hadrian restored many monuments and rebuilt the Pantheon, a temple dedicated to all the gods. He may have taken part in the groundbreaking design of the Pantheon's lofty concrete dome, which was crowned by a circular opening, 30 feet (9 m) across, that allowed sunlight to fill the temple's interior.

Emperors restored and built temples to beautify the empire and to glorify Rome (represented by the gods of the state)—and to show off their magnificence and generosity. Good public relations was one of the main reasons that emperors also sponsored the building of bathhouses, not only in Rome but in cities throughout the empire. Indoor plumbing was a rarity in the ancient world—it might be available in palaces and mansions, but that was it. To get clean, the majority of people in the empire's cities had to rely on the public baths. Along with bathing facilities, the great baths constructed by various emperors also offered swimming pools, gymnasiums, snack shops, libraries, meeting rooms, and pleasure gardens. They were all-purpose fitness and social centers, and Roman city dwellers were grateful to the emperors for providing them. From time to time, emperors even paid all bathers' admission fees for a day, a week, or even a month.

The public baths were places where people of different social classes mingled, and so were the **amphitheaters**. These huge structures were the scenes of open-air spectacles or entertainments that were held on holidays and other special occasions. One of the most famous buildings in the world is the Colosseum, the amphitheater begun in Rome by the emperor Vespasian.

The Pantheon still stands in Rome and is one of Italy's major tourist attractions.

With terraced seating for more than fifty thousand spectators, it was dedicated in 80 CE by Vespasian's son and successor, Titus. To celebrate the opening of the amphitheater, Titus sponsored one hundred days of gladiator combats and wild-animal fights.

Emperors also sponsored—and attended—chariot races in Rome's ancient racetrack, the Circus Maximus. Free spectacles and entertainments helped keep the city's people content by getting them out of their cramped apartments and distracting them from their problems. In the amphitheater, the **circus**, and the theater, the common people also had a chance to see their emperor and even, within certain limits, to express their honest opinions about various issues. It was worth an emperor's while to appear generous and accessible to the people, who might otherwise riot. As the teacher and **orator** Fronto wrote of the emperor Trajan:

> Because of his shrewd understanding … the emperor gave his attention even to actors and other performers on stage or on the race track or in the **arena**, since he knew that the Roman people are held in control principally by two things—free grain and shows—that political support depends as much on the entertainments as on matters of serious import, that … neglect of the entertainments brings damaging unpopularity … [and that] the shows placate everyone.

Along with understanding the importance of keeping the people of Rome entertained, Trajan enthusiastically promoted public works projects. He was responsible for paving many roads and building bridges throughout Italy. He had new harbor facilities constructed at Ostia, Rome's seaport. In the city of Rome itself, he built an aqueduct (for bringing fresh water down from the mountains), an amphitheater especially for mock sea battles, a public bath, and a multistory semicircular marketplace with room for around 170 shops, storehouses, and offices. Trajan's Market was designed by the emperor's favorite architect, Apollodorus of Damascus—one of the most admired architects in the ancient world. Apollodorus also created Trajan's **Forum**, the largest and grandest public meeting place in Rome, beautifully ornamented with gilded statues and marble in many colors.

TOWERING MONUMENTS

The achievements of emperors were often honored by special monuments, such as triumphal arches. Built of stone, these imposing structures usually featured sculpted **reliefs** that celebrated an emperor's military victories. Some

A representation of Trajan's Forum (including Trajan's Column) by painter Charles Lock Eastlake

emperors had columns erected to honor their conquests. The most famous of these is Trajan's Column, which is still standing on its original site in Trajan's Forum (in ancient times, there was a library on either side of the column). One hundred feet (30 m) tall, it was made from twenty huge blocks of marble and originally had a statue of the emperor on top. The entire surface was covered with reliefs illustrating Trajan's conquest of Dacia (modern Romania). This visual record begins at the bottom of the column and spirals upward in twenty-three bands of sculpted pictures that can be "read" almost like a wordless comic strip.

A different kind of military monument was built by Trajan's successor, Hadrian. On a visit to the province of Britain in 122, the emperor ordered the building of a stone wall across what is now northern England to protect the Roman territory south of the wall from raids by tribes living in what is now Scotland. The wall was about 76 miles (122 km) long, 8 to 10 feet (2.4 to 3 m) thick, and took nearly ten years to build. It was fortified by lookout towers and **milecastles**, small forts roughly 1 mile (1.6 km) apart. Hadrian's successor, Antoninus Pius, pushed Roman rule northward and had a 36-mile (58 km) earthen wall built at the new boundary. After about ten years, though, the Antonine Wall was abandoned, and Hadrian's Wall once more marked the northernmost limit of the Roman Empire.

Artifacts of Authority

Though emperors varied in ruling styles and personal tastes, impressive building projects were a favorite of ancient Rome's rulers. Sometimes these projects had religious significance. Other times an emperor's pet project made day-to-day life easier for his citizens. Much of the most interesting archaeological evidence we have stems from emperors' vanity projects.

Excavations of these sites, including Hadrian's Wall, even continue today. It's safe to say that Roman emperors succeeded in creating lasting monuments to their power.

THE EMPEROR'S IMAGE

Thanks to television, newspapers, magazines, and the internet, our leaders are familiar faces to us. The Roman emperors also wanted their faces to be familiar to the people they governed, but they had no mass media to rely on. They had to find other means, one of which was sculpture. Every emperor had himself portrayed in marble (and sometimes in bronze)—in full-length statues, in portrait busts, and in reliefs carved on buildings and monuments. Statues and busts were sent out to all parts of the empire. A single emperor's statues might portray him in a variety of ways, some of them chosen to suit specific parts of the empire: the great conqueror, the divine ruler, the philosophical thinker, the bearer of the burdens of government.

Money made the emperors' faces even more familiar to the people of the empire, for every emperor issued coins with his portrait on them. On one side of the coin the emperor was seen in profile, often with an inscription giving some or all of his titles (emperors had so many titles that they usually had to be abbreviated). The other side of the coin gave the emperor the opportunity to express a message to the people. The design might include a deity that was important to the emperor or a **personification** of a particular virtue or quality, such as Victory or Discipline. Other designs on coins referred in words or pictures to specific achievements, such as conquests and building programs. Some emperors used their coins to really get their message across: some of Hadrian's coins, for instance, refer to him as "the enricher of the world."

CHAPTER THREE

LIFE AT COURT

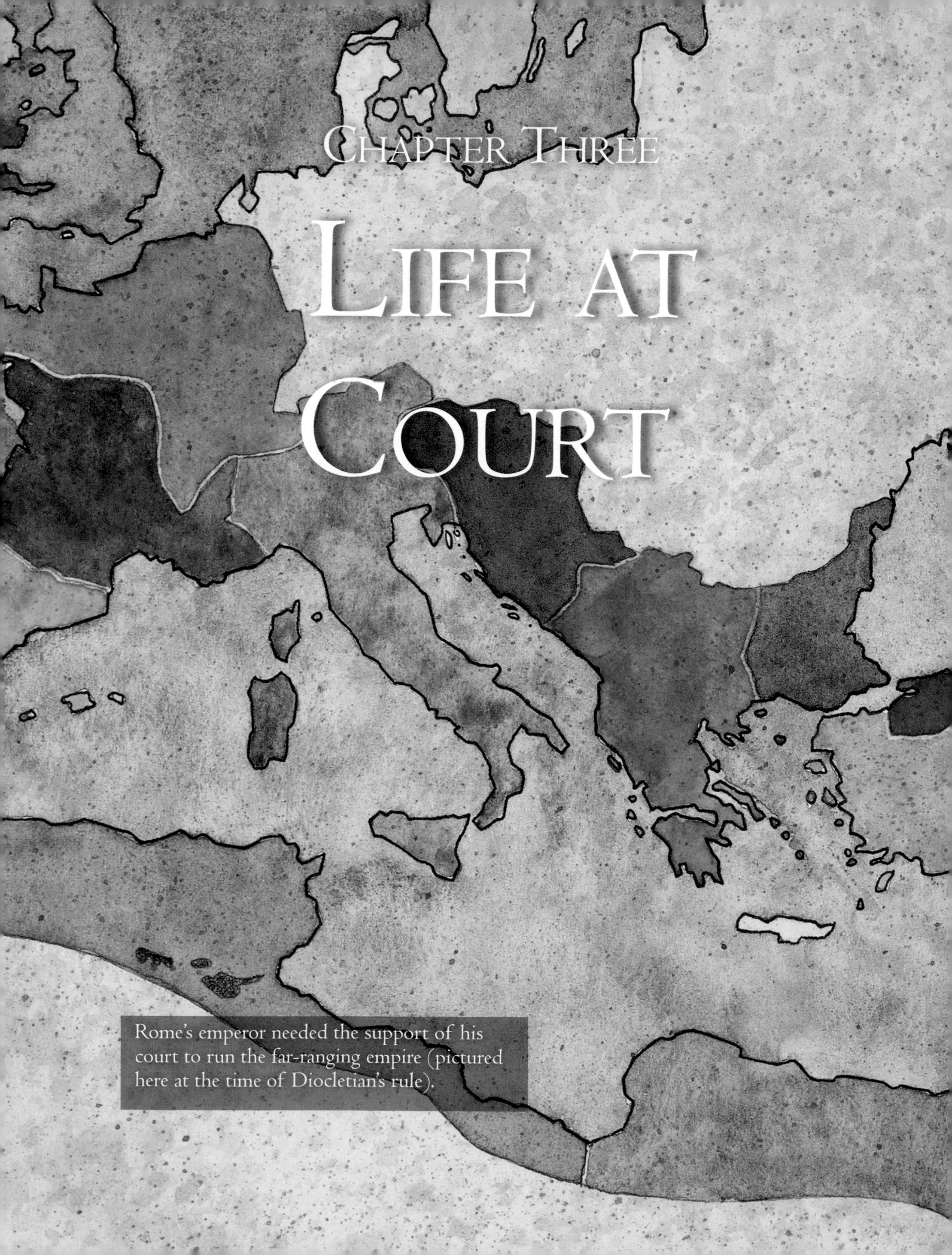

Rome's emperor needed the support of his court to run the far-ranging empire (pictured here at the time of Diocletian's rule).

"We were in the middle of these elegant trifles when Trimalchio himself was carried in to the sound of music, and was bolstered up among a host of tiny cushions, a sight that set one or two indiscreet guests laughing."

—Gaius Petronius

Emperors ruled from their palaces, from farther afield during military campaigns, or, like Hadrian (who traveled for twelve years of his twenty-one year reign), from the far reaches of the empire. The emperor oversaw a wide range of matters from wherever he was.

The emperor was the supreme judge in all legal cases involving Roman citizens—the final court of appeal. Foreign policy was his responsibility, and he met with ambassadors to discuss border issues, trade agreements, and the like. Much of his time was spent on correspondence, for he had to supervise and advise provincial governors and other officials all over the empire. And of course, he was commander in chief of the military. Naturally, the emperor's court was filled with men of many ranks who assisted him in his various duties. These courtiers understood that it was possible to rise in stature through the emperor's favor.

TRUSTED ADVISORS

The emperor generally had an informal council made up of men whom he knew well and trusted. Such men did not usually live at court but were summoned when the emperor wanted to discuss important issues and decisions with them. Because of their experience and good judgment, he could turn to them for reliable advice. These friends and supporters were most often senators, but sometimes they belonged to the next highest Roman rank, the **equites**, or equestrians. An important member of Augustus's court, for example, was the equestrian Maecenas. He was also a well-known **patron** of literature, and through him some of Rome's greatest poets became part of the emperor's circle.

Writers, in fact, belonged to the courts of a number of emperors. At the beginning of Nero's reign, one of his top advisers was the playwright and philosopher Seneca the Younger. Later, Nero chose the novelist Petronius as, in the words of Tacitus, "one of his few intimate associates, as a critic in matters of taste, while the emperor thought nothing charming or elegant in luxury unless Petronius had expressed to him his approval of it." Suetonius, who wrote biographies of emperors and other illustrious men, was chief librarian and palace secretary to Trajan. He continued in this position for a time under Hadrian, but after a few years he was dismissed for being disrespectful to the empress. Among Hadrian's friends and courtiers were philosophers, musicians, poets, mathematicians, and others. Galen, a man of many talents, served the emperors Marcus Aurelius, Commodus, and Septimius Severus as imperial physician. Galen also wrote works on philosophy, literature, grammar, and especially, medicine—in fact, his medical writings went on to become the standard textbooks for doctors throughout medieval Europe.

Augustus's good friend Maecenas loved poetry. He was an amateur poet himself, but his real gift was in recognizing and encouraging the talent of others. He gave generous financial support to such men and even brought them to the emperor's attention. Virgil, Horace, and Propertius—three of Rome's greatest poets—were all patronized by Maecenas and Augustus.

Maecenas suggested to each of these three that they write an **epic** celebrating the princeps's achievements. Propertius responded with a witty poem in which he listed the deeds of Augustus that he would have included in an epic if he had been able to compose such a long, heroic poem—but after all, he concluded, he was really best at writing love poetry. Horace had also declared that he was not an epic poet, but he did write a number of shorter poems that praised Augustus. Virgil, however, early on promised that someday he would indeed write an epic. When he did, he produced one of the finest works of Latin literature, the *Aeneid*. And although the subject of the poem was Augustus's legendary heroic ancestor Aeneas, and not the princeps himself, Virgil still managed to glorify Augustus in a way that satisfied everyone.

Then there was Ovid, Rome's most popular poet during the reign of Augustus. Ovid had little or no contact with the court, yet the emperor couldn't help but notice him. Ovid was witty and irreverent, and he wrote many poems that poked fun at or flaunted the strict, old-fashioned values that Augustus promoted. The emperor was not amused. Even though Ovid ended his great, epic-length mythological poem *Metamorphoses* with Julius Caesar's transformation into a god, Augustus must have felt that most of Ovid's poetry was extremely immoral. Eventually the emperor sent him into exile, where he spent the rest of his life because of, as Ovid himself said, "a poem and a mistake."

Naturally, men of action often played a prominent role at court. For example, Augustus's closest friend and adviser was Marcus Agrippa, a skilled general. He was born a **plebeian**, or commoner, but through his own skill and intelligence rose to great influence. He supported and fought for Augustus during the civil wars, and afterward held many important government posts. He also founded the city of Cologne, Germany, as a settlement for retiring soldiers, and he sponsored a number of important building projects in Rome. Augustus thought so much of Agrippa that he even had him marry his daughter Julia, his only child.

PROTECTING THE EMPEROR

The emperor's bodyguards played a very important role at court. Known as the **Praetorian Guard**, for most of the first two centuries of the empire it numbered around five thousand men. Praetorian soldiers took turns at guard duty in the imperial palace (receiving the watchword from the emperor himself) and protected the emperor wherever he went. If the emperor went to war, usually the whole Praetorian Guard accompanied him—they were an elite fighting force as well as bodyguards.

Unlike soldiers in the legions, who were recruited from all over the Roman world, nearly all the Praetorians came from Italy. From the reign of Tiberius on, they were stationed in a camp on the northeast edge of Rome. Each member of the guard was required to serve for twelve years (later increased to sixteen). The Praetorians were the highest paid soldiers in the empire, and they often received bonus payments from the emperors. Their special uniforms—with shining breastplates, plumed helmets, and oval shields—also set them apart from ordinary Roman soldiers.

Rome's Documentarian: Pliny the Younger

Pliny the Younger is still a well-known writer today, though he lived from 61 to 113 CE. Born Gaius Plinius Caecilius Secundus, Pliny the Younger was the nephew and adopted son of Pliny the Elder, another famous Roman. Pliny the Younger carefully recorded his wide-ranging experiences of living as a patrician in ancient Rome. He published nine volumes of writing, served as a senator, and even advised Trajan.

His letters to Trajan provide a unique look at the political wrangling of the age:

The experience, most excellent Emperor, I have had of your unbounded generosity to me, in my own person, encourages me to hope I may be yet farther obliged to it, in that of my friends. Voconius Romanus (who was my schoolfellow and companion from our earliest years) claims the first rank in that number; in consequence of which I petitioned your sacred father to promote him to the dignity of the senatorial order. But the completion of my request is reserved to your goodness; for his mother had not then advanced, in the manner the law directs, the liberal gift of [$16,000] which she engaged to give him, in her letter to the late emperor, your father. This, however, by my advice she has since done … The difficulties therefore being removed which deferred the gratification of our wishes, it is with full confidence I venture to assure you of the worth of my friend Romanus … Let me, then, entreat you, Sir, to enable me to congratulate Romanus on so desirable an occasion, and at the same time to indulge an eager and, I hope, laudable ambition, of having it in my power to boast that your favorable regards are extended not only to myself, but also to my friend.

Members of the Praetorian Guard in full regalia

The imperial bodyguards were commanded by an officer called the Praetorian prefect. He was chosen by the emperor from among the equestrians—this was one of the two top positions that men from that class could fill. (The other top post for equites was governor of Egypt, also appointed by the emperor.) Many ambitious equestrians strove for the emperor's recognition in the hope of someday becoming Praetorian prefect. A man who reached this goal could enjoy immense power and influence. For instance, Tiberius's Praetorian prefect Sejanus virtually ruled the empire for five years while the emperor lived in semi-retirement on the island of Capri. The Praetorian Guard sometimes was more interested in protecting its own interests than in protecting an emperor. The Praetorians might fail to support a new emperor who did not pay them a bonus at the beginning of his reign. Several emperors who abused their power were murdered by members of the guard. The Praetorian Guard could also play a role in selecting a new emperor when there was no clear successor. Most famously, after Praetorian officers

Patricians in the Roman Empire

In this 1881 painting by Lawrence Alma-Tadema, Claudius fears for his life after Caligula's assassination.

assassinated Gaius Caligula, they found his uncle Claudius hiding behind a curtain in the palace. The soldiers whisked him away to the Praetorian camp and proclaimed him emperor. With their loyalty sealed by huge bribes, members of the Senate were forced to accept the Praetorians' choice and voted to give Claudius all the privileges and powers of emperor.

A Crafty Courtier

Some emperors could be easily swayed or deceived by the flattery and cunning of their courtiers. Tiberius placed perfect trust in his energetic and efficient Praetorian prefect, Sejanus, honoring him by making him a senator and a consul. The emperor became so reliant on Sejanus that he referred to him as "my partner in toil." But, as the historian Tacitus described him, Sejanus was not the loyal, upright subject he appeared to be:

> He won the heart of Tiberius so effectually by various artifices that the emperor, ever dark and mysterious towards others, was with Sejanus alone careless and freespoken … He had a body which could endure hardships, and a daring spirit. He was one who screened himself, while

he was attacking others; he was as cringing as he was imperious; before the world he affected humility; in his heart he lusted after supremacy, for the sake of which he was sometimes lavish and luxurious, but oftener energetic and watchful, qualities quite as mischievous when hypocritically assumed for the attainment of sovereignty.

Eventually Sejanus's deeds caught up with him. He had been responsible for murdering or exiling several members of the imperial family, including the men who were most likely to succeed Tiberius. Although Sejanus controlled all access to the emperor, who was living in seclusion on the island of Capri, Tiberius's sister-in-law Antonia managed to get a letter to him. She warned him about the Praetorian prefect's plans to rule the empire himself, and Tiberius at last became suspicious. The emperor secretly selected a new Praetorian prefect and gave him orders to arrest and kill Sejanus, whose ambitions ended in ruin.

THE ROLE OF SLAVES

The imperial household included hundreds of slaves. Many of them performed the physical work of cleaning the palace, maintaining the gardens, laundering the emperor's togas, and so on. There were also skilled, highly trained slaves, such as cooks, physicians, and secretaries. Entertainers, both women and men, who lived at or visited the emperor's court were generally slaves, too. Among the slaves who took care of the emperor's personal needs were masseurs, barbers, and bedroom attendants (whose duties included making the bed, emptying and cleaning the chamber pot, and laying out the emperor's clothes for the day). Female slaves also lived in the palace to perform similar tasks for the women of the emperor's family.

Slaves who did their jobs well were often rewarded with their freedom. They still owed service and loyalty to the emperor, however, and often continued in their former jobs. Much of the day-to-day work of government administration was done by the imperial household's slaves and **freedmen**. Many were involved in keeping records and accounts and in writing up the emperor's correspondence. Some had very specialized jobs, such as the **nomenclator**, a kind of herald whose job was to announce the name of each person who came to visit the emperor.

The emperor's personal attendants had more contact with him than almost anyone else. Naturally a closeness often developed between the emperor and these servants. He might confide in them and ask them for their advice. Because of their personal connection, these men could be quite influential, becoming close advisers of the emperor. Claudius was especially well known for relying on his freedmen and entrusting them with government matters. He especially favored his chief secretary, Narcissus, and his financial secretary, Pallas.

LIFE AT THE TOP

It could be difficult for an emperor to know whom to trust. His courtiers were his most prized advisors. And while many emperors seemed to listen only to their own instincts, by and large the imperial court helped to balance out the whims of the emperor. Many of the most lasting records we have from ancient Rome stem from courtiers' accounts of their own lives. The next chapter explores the lives of patrician men, not as courtiers but as individuals in charge of families.

PATRICIAN MEN

While some notable Roman women appeared on coins, the vast majority of Roman currency bears likenesses of the powerful men who ruled.

"What treaty, what oath, have they not trampled under foot? We should not imitate them, the gentleman says."
—Appian, on the contrast between noble Romans and the Carthaginians

Rome was a man's world, and patrician men enjoyed the best the empire had to offer. Along with their privileges, men at the peak of Roman society were expected to use their resources to help others. Patrician men often paid large sums of money to fund building projects, entertain their friends, and help those who were less fortunate. These financial gestures did more than their stated aim: patrician men's support of the plebeians, women, and slaves helped to maintain order in the empire.

Building a successful career took more than money, though. Men in leadership were required to be excellent communicators—arguing court cases, issuing orders, giving speeches, and writing letters and reports. Skill in the use of language was a sign of success in the Roman world—and any man who wanted to be a success had to have that skill.

THE EMPEROR'S EVERYDAY LIFE

The everyday business of the empire required the emperor to spend much of his time reading and writing letters, and composing, delivering, or listening to speeches. Some emperors were famous for multitasking: Augustus would dictate letters while being shaved or having his hair cut. The *Augustan Histories* remarked that Hadrian "wrote, dictated, listened, and, incredible as it seems, conversed with his friends, all at one and the same time." Emperors generally also attended meetings in the Senate house on a regular basis and sat in judgment at trials.

Of course, work did not take up all an emperor's time. Like everyone else, an emperor had to eat, and dinner was often an occasion for enjoying a banquet and entertainment. Bathing, too, occupied an important place in nearly every Roman's day. Although the palace had its own bath facilities, some emperors, such as Titus and Hadrian, were singled out for praise because they used public baths.

As we have already seen, emperors also mingled with "the common crowd" in the theater, amphitheater, and circus. Some of Rome's rulers were not willing to be just spectators, however. Commodus shocked the Senate and common people alike by fighting as a gladiator in the arena. Gaius Caligula was so fond of chariot racing that he gave his favorite racehorse, Incitatus, "a stall of marble, a manger of ivory, purple blankets and a collar of precious stones, … a house, a troop of slaves and furniture"; he even invited Incitatus to palace banquets. Nero took part in public races as a charioteer. He also fancied himself a singer and actor and performed both on a private stage in the palace and in public theaters. A favorite courtier, the general—and future emperor—Vespasian, was once dismissed from court for falling asleep during one of Nero's long musical performances.

Some emperors cultivated their intellectual and artistic tastes more successfully. Claudius wrote histories (which have not survived to the present) and invented three new letters of the alphabet. Marcus Aurelius was a philosopher; his *Meditations*, written in Greek, is still a classic. Hadrian was the most wide-ranging of all in his interests and talents: he was said to be an expert in painting, arithmetic, geometry, and astrology; he sang, played the flute, and wrote poetry; and he enjoyed taking part in philosophical and literary debates. At the same time, he was extremely fond of hunting and was skilled in the use of a wide variety of weapons.

RISING IN THE RANKS

Hadrian, like a number of other emperors, began his career in the same manner as other high-born Roman males. He joined the army at the age of fifteen, then three years later was appointed to sit on a ten-judge panel that decided on matters of inheritance. After serving on this court, he received his first posting as a military tribune. This meant that he was second-in-command of a legion, working with the legate, or commander, and handling much of the legion's legal business. Hadrian was tribune of two different legions in turn (stationed first in what is now Hungary, then in what is now Bulgaria), before taking his first public office as quaestor.

Numerous quaestors served at once, playing various administrative and financial roles in the empire. They were involved in record keeping, worked in the treasury, and handled financial matters for provincial governors and generals in the field. Once a man had been quaestor, he automatically became a member of the Senate.

In the typical senator's career, the office of quaestor was followed by that of praetor. Praetors were judges in cases of civil law and also had responsibilities involving festivals and public games. An ex-praetor was eligible to be appointed as a legionary legate, a post he usually held for three or four years. After this he could spend a year as governor of one of the lesser provinces

A Day in the Life of Vespasian

Like most upper-class Romans, emperors often enjoyed a leisurely pace in their daily lives. This was true even of the emperors who took their responsibilities most seriously, such as Vespasian. The historian Suetonius describes for us Vespasian's "daily routine while emperor":

> He rose early, even while it was still dark. Then, after reading his letters and abstracts of official reports, he let in his friends, and while they chatted to him put on his shoes himself and got dressed. When he had dealt with any business that cropped up, he would find time for a drive and then a lie down ... After that he had a bath and then went through to dinner; it is said that he was at his most approachable and amenable at that time, so his household were eager to seize the opportunity of asking him something then.

under the Senate's control. Then, if he had the emperor's favor, he would generally be put in charge of one of the emperor's provinces—but not one where more than a single legion was stationed.

The next step up the ladder was consul—as always, with the emperor's approval. Although consuls had very little power or responsibility under the emperors, most senators still found it an honor to hold the office. After a man had served as consul, the Senate might appoint him to a one-year term as governor of Africa (modern Tunisia and northwestern Libya) or Asia (today western Turkey), the greatest provinces under the Senate's control. Or the emperor could send him to govern a province with two or more legions, and he would stay in this office for as long as the emperor wished. Gnaeus Julius Agricola (father-in-law of the historian Tacitus) was governor of the province of Britain for seven or eight years, a fairly long time.

Patricians in the Roman Empire

Between these various posts, many of which took him to the provinces, a man would spend periods at home in Rome, participating in the meetings of the Senate. He might also practice law, but senators were not allowed to engage in business. They could, however, invest in real estate, merchant expeditions, and similar moneymaking enterprises. Quite a few senators—among them the historians Tacitus and Dio Cassius—also devoted a good portion of their time to literature.

VIRTUOUS MEN

From the time of the early republic, noble Roman men were expected to live up to certain standards. Their highest calling was to serve the state, in both war and peace. The greatest virtues they could have, therefore, were *gravitas*, *pietas*, and *virtus*. These Latin words stood for concepts that were somewhat different from the meanings of the modern English words ("gravity," "piety," and "virtue") that descend from them. Gravitas basically meant "dignity," or "seriousness," and Roman noblemen and rulers were generally concerned to behave in as dignified a manner as possible, which would inspire the respect of others. Pietas referred to properly doing one's duty to parents, country, and the gods. Virtus comes from the word *vir*, "man," so literally means "manliness"—which to the Romans involved a combination of bravery, discipline, and self-sacrifice.

Virtus was first and foremost a military virtue. The Romans had always felt that military experience was essential for men in the upper classes. The leaders of the state had to have the ability to command, and the army was the best place to learn and practice this. Many reigning emperors made a point of giving their heirs a good taste of army life, as Trajan did with Hadrian. Not only did this help develop virtus, but it was the best way to earn the respect and loyalty of the legions. A man who had shared the hardships of camp life with the soldiers and led them to victory would sit all the more securely on his throne. And of course, army service in young

Emperors knew that their power was precarious without the loyalty of the army.

manhood prepared the future emperor for his role as commander in chief.

Some emperors were more interested in military matters than others. Neither Gaius Caligula nor Nero ever led the army, and Claudius took no active military role in the invasion of Britain that he ordered. Vespasian became emperor because of his success as a general and his popularity with the troops, but after taking the throne he left active military command to his son Titus. Hadrian, on the other hand, was one of the emperors who was closely involved with the army both before and after coming to the throne. On a visit to Germany as emperor, Hadrian made a point of spending time among the legions stationed there. According to the *Augustan Histories*:

> Though more desirous of peace than of war, he kept the soldiers in training just as if war were imminent, inspired them by proofs of his own powers of endurance, actually led a soldier's life among [them] … and, after the example of … his own adoptive father Trajan, cheerfully ate out of doors such camp-fare as bacon, cheese, and vinegar … He incited others by the example of his own soldiery spirit; he would walk as much as twenty miles fully armed; he … generally wore the commonest clothing, would have no gold ornaments on his swordbelt or jewels on the clasp … [He] visited the sick soldiers in their quarters, selected the sites for camps, … banished luxuries on every hand, and, lastly, improved the soldiers' arms and equipment … He made it a point to be acquainted with the soldiers and to know their numbers.

Patricians in the Roman Empire

For the Fatherland

One of the clearest expressions of what virtus, or manliness, meant to upper-class Romans can be found in a poem from Horace's third book of *Odes*. The poem is untitled in Latin, but English translators sometimes call it "Discipline." Here are some selections from it:

> Let the vigorous boy learn well to bear
> Lean hardship like a friend in bitter war,
> And let the fearsome man on horse
> With his spear harass the fierce Parthian force.
>
> ...
>
> It is sweet and fitting to die for the fatherland.
> Besides, death hunts down a fleeing man
> And for unwarlike youth shows no mercy
> To cowardly back or bended knees.
>
>
> Virtus, never knowing disgraceful defeat,
> Shines with untarnished pride and respect
> And neither takes up nor lays down its power
> At the pleasure of the people's changing favor.

These passages make it clear that living up to expectations was a tall order for patrician men.

CHAPTER FIVE

PATRICIAN WOMEN

This bust of a Roman woman is part
of the Louvre's permanent collection.

"Did you know that the sad journey is lifted from your girl's mind? / I am allowed to spend my birthday now at Rome."
—Lines from a poem by Sulpicia

The expectations of patrician women were vastly different from those of patrician men. Whereas men achieved status through education and their careers, a patrician woman was considered successful if she ran her household effectively. Tasks such as buying the family's food fell to the woman of the house. Opportunities for patrician women outside of becoming a wife and mother were slim. However, there were instances of unmarried women landowners who had more autonomy than their married counterparts. Other exceptions to the typical patrician lifestyle included women who served as priestesses or owned their own businesses.

Although women could not vote, those who married men of high rank exercised power indirectly. Sometimes their influence went unnoticed. Other times their power had the same deadly consequences as patrician men faced.

A Patriarchal Society

Roman society was set up to put all power in the hands of men. The male head of the family had absolute authority over all his children, and often over grandchildren and other relatives as well. He decided whom they married and could also order them to divorce for any reason he pleased. (Under Roman law, children remained with their father after a divorce.) He could disown family members and punish them harshly for misbehavior. All the family finances were controlled by him, and his consent was necessary for most major decisions made by other family members. This *patria potestas*, or "power of the father," was especially dominant in the lives of women, who could never become the heads of families.

The law generally required that a woman always have a male guardian, normally her father or husband, for her entire life. If he died, the courts would appoint another guardian. A woman could not handle financial, business, or legal matters without her guardian's permission and assistance. From the time of Augustus, however, the law allowed a mother of three children to be freed from guardianship.

The first emperor was very disturbed by new trends he observed in Roman society. People were often staying unmarried, or marrying later in life, or not having children when they did marry, especially in the upper class. Augustus wanted to change this situation to strengthen the family and keep it at the center of society. He created laws that rewarded people for having three or more children, punished them (by reducing their right to inherit property) for remaining unmarried or childless, and required women to remarry after being widowed or divorced. These laws also tried to control other aspects of women's and men's private lives.

In spite of the legislation, the birth rate among the upper class does not seem to have increased. This is partly because pregnancy and childbirth were extremely risky for women in ancient times. Even with the best health care, many diseases and problems were not preventable, and there were few medical techniques that could help a woman if something went wrong during pregnancy or birth. Miscarriages were common, and many women—and their babies—died from childbirth complications. Very often, parents who dearly wanted to have many children just were not able to. Among such parents was Augustus himself. His only child was his daughter, Julia, from his second marriage.

A Daughter Ruled by Her Father

Augustus was an old-fashioned father and insisted that his daughter, Julia, spend her time spinning and weaving like the virtuous Roman women of earlier days. (Julia and her stepmother made most of the emperor's clothes themselves.) She was strictly supervised, seldom allowed to go out, and was not allowed to have any boyfriends.

Like many upper-class Roman daughters, Julia was at the mercy of her father's ambitions. At the age of fourteen, Augustus had her marry his nephew Marcellus, who was in his late teens at the time. The young man died two years later, in 23 BCE, leaving no children behind. Augustus was determined that Julia bear children who could succeed him, so in 21 BCE he married her to his friend Agrippa—after making Agrippa divorce the wife he already had. Agrippa was twenty-five years older than Julia, but they had five children together, and Augustus adopted the two oldest boys to be his heirs.

When Agrippa died in 12 BCE, the emperor worried about who would be his heirs' guardian if he should die. He forced his stepson Tiberius to divorce his wife, whom he loved deeply, and early in the next year Julia was married to him. Tiberius never came to love—or even like—Julia, and life at court was unpleasant for him in other ways. With Augustus's permission, he left Rome and Julia (five years after their wedding) to live on the Greek island of Rhodes.

Julia took the opportunity to rebel against her strict upbringing and her arranged marriages. Roman authors later exaggerated her misconduct, but she certainly did not uphold her father's ideas about proper moral behavior for women. In 2 BCE, after denouncing her to the entire Senate, Augustus condemned Julia to exile. She died in despair fifteen years later, not long after her father's death.

Secret Influence

Augustus divorced his second wife to marry Livia, who belonged to one of Rome's oldest and most influential noble families. She was already married and was pregnant with her second child, but the emperor ordered her husband to divorce her. After that, according to Suetonius, Livia was "the one woman he truly loved until his death." Augustus certainly valued her, trusting her to meet with ambassadors when he was busy with other matters. He not only asked her for advice on a regular basis but also took notes on what she said so that he could study it later. When Livia's son Tiberius succeeded to the throne, Livia expected her influence to continue. The new emperor, however, felt that his mother was constantly interfering with affairs that shouldn't concern her, and he resented her for it. For good or ill, she remained a powerful force at court until her death at the unusually ripe old age of eighty-six.

Livia set a pattern for many of the imperial women of the first century. Proud of their descent from Augustus or from ancient noble families, a number of them were strong-willed and eager to play a part in ruling the empire. Their actions were always unofficial, of course, since no Roman woman could hold office or even vote. But simply through their closeness to the emperor, they could achieve great influence.

Gaius Caligula, for example, was an extremely unstable man, but his sister Drusilla was able to keep him from getting too out of hand until her death in the second year of his reign. His youngest sister, Agrippina, eventually married his successor, Claudius. She was able to take on some official duties (scandalizing many Romans), appearing in civic ceremonies and publicly receiving ambassadors in a way that even Livia had not done. Agrippina also schemed to have her son, Nero, made the emperor's heir. She was willing to use any means necessary—including having Claudius poisoned when she feared he would put a stop to her plans.

On Nero's first day as emperor, the password he gave to the Praetorian Guard was "best of mothers." His mother was the dominant influence on his life, and at first he was devoted to her. But it seemed that what she really wanted was to rule the empire through her son. Before long, Nero was fed up with her interference and refused to let her live in the palace any longer. Then, his frustration turning to hatred, Nero arranged to have Agrippina killed. Tacitus related, "Many years before, Agrippina had anticipated this end for herself … For when she consulted the astrologers about Nero, they replied that he would be emperor and kill his mother. 'Let him kill her,' she said, 'provided he is emperor.'"

After the reign of Nero, empresses and other women of the imperial family generally seem to have exercised their influence more quietly—and more peacefully. Titus's daughter, Julia Titi, for example, suggested to her father the nomination of a particular man for consul. Trajan's wife, Plotina, was sometimes criticized for the determination with which she arranged for Hadrian to succeed her husband. More often, though, she was praised for being a model of womanly modesty and virtue. She is known to have advised both Trajan and Hadrian in political matters, and her advice was valued.

Plotina also encouraged her husband to marry his great-niece Sabina to Hadrian. This marriage may not have been a very happy one—Hadrian complained about Sabina's moodiness—but the two worked well together as emperor and empress, if not as husband and wife. We know that Sabina accompanied Hadrian on at least some of his travels: her friend Julia Balbilla, a Greek noblewoman, inscribed a poem on the leg of an ancient Egyptian statue to commemorate the empress's visit to Egypt.

THE LIFESTYLE OF PATRICIAN WOMEN

Perhaps one of the happiest of all imperial marriages was that of Antoninus Pius and Annia Galeria Faustina. The emperor once said of his wife, "By heaven, I would rather live with her on Gyara [in exile] than in the palace without her." Many husbands and wives had similar feelings. Even though all upper-class Roman marriages were arranged and involved **dowry** negotiations, the spouses often grew to love and respect each other. Divorce was common and easy to obtain, and people often remarried after being widowed. But the ideal for both men and women was still felt to be lifelong marriage to one person. An upper-class husband, speaking at his wife's funeral in about 10 CE, said, "Rare indeed are marriages of such long duration, which are ended by death, not divorce. We had the good fortune to spend forty-one years together with no unhappiness."

In this same **eulogy**, the husband praised his wife for excelling in traditional womanly qualities: "your modesty, obedience, affability, and good nature, your tireless attention to wool-working, your performance of religious duties without superstitious fear, your artless elegance and simplicity of dress … your affection toward your relatives, your sense of duty toward your family." This wife was so devoted to her husband that when she found she couldn't have children, she offered to let him divorce her so that he could try to have them with someone else. He answered that his hope for children could never match his commitment to her.

Roman women wore togas early in the empire; later they wore tunics.

As this eulogy indicates, household duties and, if possible, raising children were an upper-class woman's main responsibilities. A number of slaves and sometimes freedwomen helped her with these tasks. In addition, upper-class women had slaves to style their hair, take care of their clothes and cosmetics, and escort them through the streets.

Roman women were able to go out to visit friends, go to the baths, attend banquets and birthday parties, take part in religious ceremonies (some for women only), and watch plays and public shows. At home, a Roman lady might fill her leisure hours with reading, writing or dictating letters to friends, or playing a musical instrument like the **lyre**.

A wealthy woman could benefit her family and community by using her inheritance to provide dowries for poor female relatives or funding the construction of a temple or other public building. One elderly lady who used some of her money for good causes such as these also used her wealth

A variety of hairstyles were popular in ancient Rome.

and leisure to indulge her love for popular entertainment. Although this behavior rather shocked the conservative writer Pliny, he praised her for making sure that her pleasures didn't keep her grandson from developing proper Roman gravitas:

> Ummidia Quadratilla … owned a company of **pantomime** dancers and enjoyed their performances with more enthusiasm than was proper for a woman of her social rank. However, her grandson Quadratus, who was brought up in her household, never saw their performances, either in the theater or at home … She herself told me … that she, during the idle hours which women have, used to relax by playing checkers or watching pantomimes; but when she was about to do either, she always told her grandson to go and study.

WOMEN ADORNED

Many artifacts remain today that demonstrate the particular care with which patrician women dressed. Women of the upper class wore tunics, cloaks, and dresses. The fabric of these garments distinguished them from lower-class women: patricians favored silk and imported cotton. Women's dress merely began with their clothes—accessories, perfumes, and cosmetics rounded out their look. Jewelry was commonly crafted from gold, bronze, and precious stones. Perhaps the most interesting kind of accessories were hairpieces, which were much like today's hair extensions. Sometimes even marble busts had a hairstyle made from a separate piece of marble so that it could be updated as styles changed! Archaeologist Elizabeth Bartman points out that the hairstyles of these sculptures have helped historians determine the identity of the woman depicted:

> In ancient Rome hair was a major determinant of a woman's physical
> attractiveness and was thus deemed worthy of considerable exertions
> to create a flattering appearance. Just as every face had its own [distinct
> facial features]; so did female hairstyles vary—along with looks, a
> woman's age, social status, and public role influenced her choice of
> coiffure. This variety has proved invaluable in identifying historical
> individuals, thereby enabling scholars to construct a chronology of
> Roman portraiture and, by extension, Roman art.

Chapter Six

Children of the Ruling Class

Education in Rome centered around reading, writing, and basic math.

"Here boys are turned into men.
Give them a long sojourn in our city …"
—Juvenal

Childhood in ancient Rome lasted only a short time. Yet for patrician children, youth was a time both to learn and to play. Much like the adults of the upper class, boys and girls had different responsibilities within their families. Girls' lives revolved largely around the home, while boys eventually pursued further education in schools. Patrician fathers generally preferred sons to daughters, but wealthy families (who did not have to worry about having too many mouths to feed) were usually overjoyed by the birth of any healthy child.

BIRTH AND THE INFANT YEARS

All Roman babies were born at home. Nine days after birth, a ceremony of purification was held to protect the baby from evil. Then the child was formally named and given a **bulla**, a good luck charm often made of gold. Occasionally, parents went even further to try to guarantee good fortune for their newborn.

Gaius Caligula, for instance, carried his baby daughter Julia Drusilla to every temple of every goddess in Rome so that she would be blessed by them all.

Sometimes, even when a baby was born healthy, the mother did not survive childbirth. The father would then hire a wet nurse to breastfeed the baby. Some healthy Roman mothers felt that breastfeeding was beneath their dignity, and so their children, too, might be nurtured by wet nurses. Nurses were usually slaves or freedwomen. The first-century-CE orator Quintilian recommended, "Above all, make sure that the infant's nurse speaks correctly ... Of course, she should without doubt be chosen on the basis of good moral character, but make sure that she speaks correctly as well. The child will hear his nurse first, and will learn to speak by imitating her words." A nurse often continued to care for a child after he or she was weaned, with lasting affection forming between the two.

Bullae from Herculaneum

Patricians in the Roman Empire

Another important person in a young child's life, especially a boy's, was the *paedagogus*, also a slave. His job was to rock the cradle and babysit, then to play with the child, take him on outings, and teach him table manners and perhaps the beginnings of reading and writing. As a boy grew still older, the paedagogus became a protector who escorted him to and from school, the baths, the theater, and elsewhere, shielding him from any immoral influences on the way. Many boys grew up feeling the same affection for their paedagogi as for their nurses. As an expression of gratitude, these slaves often received their freedom when their charges became adults.

Schooling and Leisure

Children of imperial and senatorial families had their choice of many toys. Among others, there were dolls, balls, tops, marbles, board games, hobbyhorses, model chariots, and (only for boys) wooden swords and shields. Some boys had miniature chariots that they could ride in, pulled by a goat.

Roman children began learning from their parents at an early age. Parents were encouraged to make learning fun and not to push too hard. They usually taught the alphabet, the basics of reading, and perhaps some simple math. What was most important, though, was for the parents to give their children a moral education. They might do this by reading or telling stories about great Roman heroes of the past so that children could learn from these famous examples of gravitas, pietas, and virtus.

Dolls could be crafted from basic materials or be more refined, like this wooden doll.

Formal education typically began at about age seven. Children of very wealthy families were generally taught at home by tutors. Augustus hired a famous teacher to move into the palace and educate his grandsons. Many other emperors had palace schools where they employed the best tutors to instruct children of the imperial family. Children of favored senators and others might also be invited to the imperial school. Claudius, for instance, rewarded Vespasian for his military service in the invasion of Britain by giving his son Titus a court education.

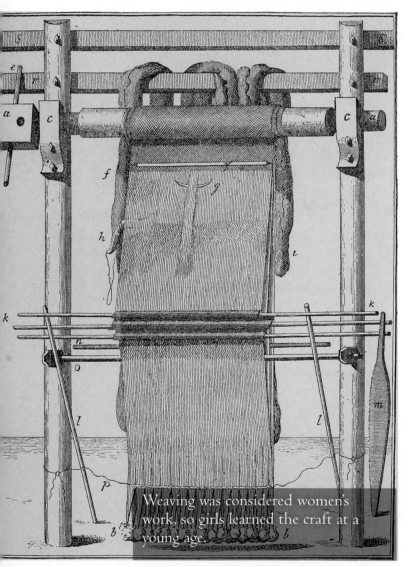

Weaving was considered women's work, so girls learned the craft at a young age.

The most important part of an upper-class boy's formal education was training in Latin and Greek, literature, and public speaking. Math was of next importance, but science was studied little, if at all. Many boys also studied philosophy, but the general opinion was that it was not proper for high-ranking Romans to be too interested in philosophy. As a boy, Hadrian was so fond of Greek literature and Greek philosophy that people nicknamed him Greekling. Hadrian didn't seem to mind and continued to love all things Greek for the rest of his life.

Many upper-class Roman boys, in fact, finished their formal education with a tour of Greece, where they could study with some of the best orators to be found.

Roman girls received much less education than boys. They did learn Latin and literature, perhaps Greek, and probably a little math. Training in public

KNUCKLEBONES

Although many toys from the Roman Empire are familiar to us today, one unusual game was wildly popular during ancient times. **Knucklebones** (or *tali* in Latin) got its name from the materials required to play the game: five actual knucklebones from sheep or goats. These bones were thrown into the air, and children tried to catch them on the back of one of their hands, with their palms facing the ground. Another method of game play involved throwing the knucklebones into a small receptacle.

Knucklebones was not just a fun pursuit for children. Men gambled on games, and historians believe that women sometimes tried to predict the future based on knucklebones' landing patterns, much like reading tea leaves. We know that knucklebones was a widespread diversion thanks to the multitude of paintings and sculptures that show players engaged in the game. These depictions are not limited to ancient Rome, though. Knucklebones existed well before ancient Rome and continued to be played long after the height of the empire.

speaking was considered unnecessary, however; household skills were much more important. While the daughters of wealthy families would never need to cook or clean for themselves, they would have to supervise the slaves who did such work, and they usually were expected to know how to spin and weave.

From Childhood to Adulthood

Childhood ended very early for upper-class girls, who could (and often did) marry as young as twelve. Their husbands were usually in at least their mid-twenties, but they might be quite a bit older, perhaps even in their fifties, having already been married once or twice. The marriage was often arranged for financial or political reasons, and the girl's feelings might not be taken into account at all. It was her duty, and part of the virtue of pietas, to gladly accept her father's choice of a husband.

An older husband often took it on himself to finish his young wife's education, perhaps polishing her manners and her appreciation of literature. For example, Pliny had a friend who, he wrote, "has recently read me some letters which he said were written by his wife … Whether they are really his wife's, as he says, or his own … one can only admire him either for what he writes, or the way he has cultivated and refined the taste of the girl he married."

Boys spent their teen years finishing their education, especially honing their public-speaking skills. Between the ages of fifteen and eighteen, it was time for the coming-of-age ceremony. An upper-class boy in Rome first went to the household shrine of his family's protector deities. There he left his bulla and his purple-bordered toga, the garment of childhood. This was replaced with the pure white toga of manhood. Then his family and friends accompanied him to the Forum, where he was formally proclaimed a citizen. After a visit to the city's most important temple, the rest of the day was spent feasting and celebrating. Once a boy came of age, he could begin his career in the military and government.

A Turbulent Childhood

Upper-class children grew up in a variety of settings and could experience huge ups and downs. Gaius Caligula is a prime example. As a young child, Caligula, along with his mother and siblings, lived in an army camp while his father was commanding the legions stationed in Germany. His parents often dressed him up in a miniature army uniform, including the tough sandals called *caligae*. Because of this, the soldiers, who were fond of him, nicknamed him Caligula. Afterward he went with his parents to his father's next posting, in Syria, but there his father died (perhaps poisoned).

When Gaius was fifteen, his second-oldest brother was arrested for treason. Two years later, his mother and oldest brother were sent into exile because the emperor Tiberius suspected them of plotting against him. By the time Gaius was twenty-one, all three were dead. Meanwhile, he briefly lived with his grandmother, then was summoned to join the emperor on Capri, where he stayed until he himself became emperor.

While Caligula's trajectory was certainly out of the ordinary, his life demonstrates that patrician children grew up fast and were expected to maneuver through society in a way that maximized their power and status.

CHAPTER SEVEN

RISKS AND REWARDS

The assassination of Julius Caesar

"Valor is of no service, chance rules all, and the bravest
often fall by the hands of cowards."
—Tacitus

Most Romans led lives far removed from the comforts of the patricians. Senatorial families and the imperial court were only a small percentage of the population. This minority controlled most of the empire's wealth. As we have seen, the patricians frequently used their wealth for the public good, from building temples and aqueducts to contributing funds to feed the poor. Like the rich and powerful of every time and place, they also spent their money on luxuries and entertainments. Those at the highest levels of power certainly enjoyed equally high privileges. At the same time, although they were secure from hunger and want, they were, like everyone else, vulnerable to illnesses and injuries. And when it came to struggles for power or the fears and whims of an unstable emperor, the patricians might pay a high price for living at the top of society.

THE GOOD LIFE

Wealthy Romans had perhaps the highest standard of living in the ancient world. Upper-class homes were spacious and beautifully decorated—and most well-off families had one or more country villas in addition to their house in Rome. With all their needs attended to by slaves, Romans at this level of society had plenty of leisure time. Literary senators liked to hold and attend recitations, where poems, histories, and other works were recited, or read aloud, often by the author himself. Others enjoyed going to gladiatorial combats, wild-animal fights, and chariot races. Everyone liked to have a good afternoon bath and massage, perhaps with an exercise session or ball game first.

After the afternoon bath came the highlight of many Romans' day: dinnertime. Although Augustus was well known for preferring plain food such as bread, herring, cheese, and green figs, very few of his successors—or other wealthy Romans—were content with such simple meals. Banquets were held frequently, with numerous courses served on silver dishes. Along with good conversation, there was usually entertainment of some kind: plays, poetry readings, music, acrobats, or dancers. Sometimes banqueters enjoyed games or a little gambling. Writing of Augustus, Suetonius related that "at some dinner parties he would auction tickets for prizes of most unequal value, and paintings with their faces turned to the wall, for which every guest present was expected to bid blindly, taking his chance like the rest: he might either pick up most satisfactory bargains, or throw away his money."

To entertain the common people, their courts, and themselves, emperors frequently produced spectacles—for example, flooding an arena and staging mock sea battles. One of the most lavish productions of all was Gaius Caligula's 2-mile (3.2 km) bridge of boats. The emperor had merchant ships line up across the Bay of Naples, and a road was built on top of them. During two days of festivities, Caligula, dressed in splendid costumes, raced across the boat-bridge, first on a fast horse and then in a two-horse chariot, accompanied by the entire Praetorian Guard and all his friends in chariots. Extravaganzas like this were impressive and enjoyed by many, but they were expensive to produce, even for an emperor. Too many spectacles of this sort would cause a drain on the imperial treasury—a sure sign of trouble coming.

EATING LIKE AN EMPEROR

Upper-class Romans often served elaborate dinners in their gardens. The guests reclined, leaning on their left elbows, on couches around a central table. People used knives for cutting meat and spoons for eating soup, but otherwise ate with their fingers. Dinnertime in ancient Rome came in late afternoon— and if dinner was a banquet, it could last for hours.

There were three parts to each dinner, and each could have many dishes. First came appetizers, then the main course, and finally dessert. Common appetizers were egg dishes, raw vegetables, and fish. The main course was meats and cooked vegetables. This was where the greatest variety and most elaborate preparation could come in. Dessert was generally fruit and pastries. The usual drink was wine, sometimes flavored with spices.

Emperors and wealthy Romans ate many exotic foods, such as sea urchins, roasted peacocks, and flamingoes' tongues. They had large staffs of well-trained slaves to cook and serve their meals.

THE PERIL OF PRIVILEGE

As we have seen, just because a man was emperor did not mean that he was indestructible. Half of the first twenty Roman emperors died from old age, strokes, or illnesses such as malaria and cancer. The other half died by violence—two committed suicide, and the rest were assassinated. The murderers were nearly always people close to the emperor: Praetorian Guardsmen, freedmen of the court, even family members.

When it came to palace plots, women could be every bit the equal of men, it seems. Two of Gaius Caligula's sisters, for example, were involved in a conspiracy to overthrow him and were sent into exile. Claudius's third wife, Messalina, schemed to marry another man and make him emperor. (We have already encountered the plotting of Claudius's fourth wife, Agrippina.) There were many rumors about women at the imperial court who poisoned possible heirs so that their own sons or favorites could succeed to the throne.

The very possibility of conspiracies afflicted some emperors severely. Tiberius retired to the island of Capri largely because he was so worried about plots against him. Toward the end of his reign, his fears led to a large number of treason trials in Rome. Nero, too, often suspected courtiers, senators, and even family members of conspiring to overthrow him. Like Tiberius, he was sometimes right. But Nero's drastic measures to deal with conspirators and potential troublemakers—executing or exiling many senators and others, sometimes on the slimmest evidence—made him even more likely to be the victim of plots.

Events like these show how dangerous it sometimes was to be part of the circle of power. Pliny the Younger lived through the reign of Domitian, another emperor whose tyrannical behavior and extreme insecurity resulted in sweeping executions. Pliny experienced the last four years of Domitian's rule and reported that several of his friends had been executed or faced banishment. He worried about his own safety during that time.

Persecutions and other acts of violence and cruelty are often the main things that many people associate with the Roman emperors. We need to balance this image, however, with the memory of emperors who governed well.

The ancient world was not perfect, and yet it has left us much that is inspiring: great works of literature, structures that have stood for two thousand years, beautiful paintings and statues, and stories of bravery, love, and devotion among people much like us.

AN OVER-THE-TOP MEAL

Some Romans at the apex of society spent more lavishly than others. The *Augustan Histories* detail a dinner party held by Marcus Aurelius's co-emperor, Lucius Verus:

One [banquet], indeed, became very notorious. This was the first banquet, it is said, at which couches were placed for twelve, although there is a very well-known saying about the proper number of those present at a banquet that "seven make a dinner, nine make a din." Furthermore … the carvers and platters, too, were presented to each [guest as a present], and also live animals either tame or wild, winged or quadruped, of whatever kind were the meats that were served, and even goblets of **murra** or of Alexandrine crystal were presented to each man for each drink, as often as they drank. Besides this, he gave golden and silver and even jeweled cups, and garlands, too, entwined with golden ribbons and flowers out of season, golden vases with ointments made in the shape of perfume-boxes, and even carriages, together with mules and muleteers, and trappings of silver, wherewith they might return home from the banquet. The estimated cost of the whole banquet, it is reported, was six million **sestertii**.

To put the cost of this meal into perspective, scholars say that a small farm cost one hundred thousand sestertii in ancient Rome.

Glossary

amphitheater

An oval stadium, mainly for shows involving combat or wild-animal fights.

aqueduct

An artificial channel to carry water from its source to a city.

arena

An amphitheater's central, ground-level area, where the amphitheater's shows took place.

Augustan Histories

A set of biographies of Roman emperors; historians believe some of these biographies might contain factual inaccuracies.

bulla

An amulet commonly worn by Roman boys from birth through their teenage years.

circus

A long, oval stadium where chariot races were held; a racetrack.

consul

An elected political position; consuls were elected in pairs to serve as the head of state.

dowry

Money and/or goods that a woman's family gave her to take into her marriage.

epic

A long poem that tells a story of a hero's accomplishments.

equites (EH-quee-tays)

Members of Rome's second-highest class, ranking below senators; in general, they were wealthy businessmen.

eulogy

A speech given at a funeral to praise the dead person; upper-class Romans often delivered eulogies in the Forum and then had them inscribed on marble.

forum

The civic center and main meeting place of a Roman city, with government buildings, offices, shops, and temples surrounding a large open area.

freedmen

Former slaves who were granted their freedom.

gladiators

Professional fighters (nearly always slaves) trained for combat in the amphitheater.

imperium

"Supreme command"—the power to command troops, interpret the law, and pass judgment (including the death sentence) on offenders.

knucklebones

A game played by Roman children and adults alike.

legate

A man who commanded armed forces on behalf of the emperor.

lyre

A stringed instrument a bit like a small harp.

milecastle

A small fort placed approximately 1 mile (1.6 km) from the next.

murra

A costly material used to craft drinking cups.

nomenclator

A job that involved announcing the arrival of guests.

orator

A person skilled in writing and making speeches.

pantomime

A ballet-like performance in which dancers, accompanied by music, wordlessly acted out stories, usually from myth or legend.

patrician

Rome's highest social class; the population from which emperors came.

patron

An upper-class Roman who gave financial support and other assistance to lower-ranking men.

personification

A deity or imaginary being that represents a thing or idea.

plebeian

A commoner, the social class to which most Romans belonged.

Praetorian Guard

The troops tasked with protecting the emperor.

princeps

"Leader" or "first citizen" in Latin; emperors from Augustus to Diocletian referred to themselves by this title.

reliefs

Sculptures in which the images project out from a flat surface.

sesterce (plural sestertii)

A Roman coin.

villas

Country estates.

FURTHER INFORMATION

BOOKS

Beard, Mary. *S.P.Q.R.: A History of Ancient Rome*. New York: Liveright Publishing, 2015.

Bunson, Matthew. *Encyclopedia of Ancient Rome*. New York: Facts on File, 2012.

Potter, David S., ed. *A Companion to the Roman Empire*. Malden, MA: Blackwell Pub., 2009.

WEBSITES

Khan Academy: Ancient Rome

https://www.khanacademy.org/test-prep/ap-art-history/ancient-mediterranean-AP/ap-ancient-rome/v/a-tour-through-ancient-rome-in-320-c-e

An in-depth lesson about how the art of ancient Rome reveals its social structure.

The Private Life of Romans

http://www.forumromanum.org/life/johnston.html

Forum Romanum hosts a digital edition of Harold Whetstone Johnston's book *The Private Life of Romans*. Content is broken down into easy-to-navigate topics and subtopics.

The Roman Empire: Patricians

http://www.pbs.org/empires/romans/empire/patricians.html

This website from PBS describes the Patrician lifestyle and also the day-to-day lives of other social classes in ancient Rome.

ORGANIZATIONS

Association of Ancient Historians

secretary@associationofancienthistorians.org

Website: http://www.associationofancienthistorians.org

The Association of Ancient Historians (AAH) is a professional organization for American and Canadian scholars who study antiquity. Membership is open to everyone with an interest in ancient history, and the group hosts yearly conferences and publishes new research in their newsletters and monograph series.

Eaton Gallery of Rome

Website: http://www.rom.on.ca/en/exhibitions-galleries/galleries/world-cultures/eaton-gallery-rome

The Royal Ontario Museum's Eaton Gallery features "the largest collection of Roman artifacts in Canada." Visitors can study Roman art, as well as objects used in everyday life.

Society for the Promotion of Roman Studies

Website: http://www.romansociety.org

The Society for the Promotion of Roman Studies was founded in 1910. The organization boasts members from over forty countries and is free to join. The Roman Society, as it's known, also hosts an online image gallery of over four thousand images.

Source Notes

Chapter 1: Emperors and the Senate

p. 7, Cassius, Dio, Earnest Cary, and Herbert Baldwin Foster. *Roman History: Books 1-11*. Vol. 1. Cambridge, MA: Harvard University Press, 1914. p. 129

p. 10, Shelton, Jo-Ann. *As the Romans Did: A Source Book in Roman Social History*. 2nd ed. New York: Oxford University Press, 1998. p. 229

p. 11, Ibid., p. 235

p. 11, Ibid., p. 228

p. 12, Boardman, John, et al., eds. *The Oxford Illustrated History of the Roman World*. New York: Oxford University Press, 1988. p. 132

p. 13, Scarre, Chris. *Chronicle of the Roman Emperors: The Reign-by-Reign Record of the Rulers of Imperial Rome.* London: Thames & Hudson, 1995. p. 95

Chapter 2: Demonstrations of Wealth and Power

p. 17, Augustus. *The Deeds of the Divine Augustus*. Translated by Thomas Bushnell. The Internet Classics Archive, 1998. Retrieved May 4, 2016. http://classics.mit.edu/Augustus/deeds.html.

p. 20, Scarre, Chris. *Chronicle of the Roman Emperors: The Reign-by-Reign Record of the Rulers of Imperial Rome*. London: Thames & Hudson, 1995. p. 102

p. 22, Shelton, Jo-Ann. *As the Romans Did: A Source Book in Roman Social History*. 2nd ed. New York: Oxford University Press, 1998. p. 334

p. 25, Editors of Time-Life *Books. Rome: Echoes of Imperial Glory*. Alexandria, VA: Time-Life Books, 1994. p. 81

Chapter 3: Life at Court

p. 27, Arbiter, Petronius. *The Satyricon*. Translated by A. R. Allinson. New York: Panurge Press, 1930. p. 302

p. 28, Mellor, Ronald, ed. *The Historians of Ancient Rome: An Anthology of the Major Writings*. New York: Routledge, 1998. p. 477

p. 29, Boardman, John, et al., eds. *The Oxford Illustrated History of the Roman World*. New York: Oxford University Press, 1988. p. 203

p. 31, Pliny. "To the Emperor Trajan." *Pliny the Younger: Letters*. The Harvard Classics. Retrieved June 07, 2016. http://www.bartleby.com/9/4/2003.

p. 33, Wells, Colin. *The Roman Empire*. 2nd ed. Cambridge, MA: Harvard University Press, 1992. p. 105

pp. 33–34, Mellor, Ronald, ed. *The Historians of Ancient Rome: An Anthology of the Major Writings*. New York: Routledge, 1998. p. 445

Chapter 4: Patrician Men

p. 37, Appian. *The Foreign Wars*. Horace White. New York. The Macmillan Company. 1899. p. 64

p. 38, Mellor, Ronald, ed. *The Historians of Ancient Rome: An Anthology of the Major Writings*. New York: Routledge, 1998. p. 506

p. 38, Ibid., p. 389

p. 40, Kamm, Antony. *The Romans: An Introduction*. New York: Routledge, 1995. pp. 68–69

p. 42, Mellor, Ronald, ed. *The Historians of Ancient Rome: An Anthology of the Major Writings*. New York: Routledge, 1998. p. 499–500

p. 43, Horace. "Odes III." Translated by the author. *The Latin Library*. Accessed May 11, 2016. http://www.thelatinlibrary.com/horace/carm3.shtml.

Chapter 5: Patrician Women

p. 45, Tibullus. *The Complete Poems of Tibullus: An En Face Bilingual Edition*. Translated by Rodney G. Dennis and Michael C. J. Putnam. Berkeley: University of California Press, 2012. p. 125

p. 48, Wells, Colin. *The Roman Empire*. 2nd ed. Cambridge, MA: Harvard University Press, 1992. p. 19

p. 49, Scarre, Chris. *Chronicle of the Roman Emperors: The Reign-by-Reign Record of the Rulers of Imperial Rome*. London: Thames & Hudson, 1995. p. 51

p. 49, Mellor, Ronald, ed. *The Historians of Ancient Rome: An Anthology of the Major Writings*. New York: Routledge, 1998. p. 470

p. 50, Scarre, Chris. *Chronicle of the Roman Emperors: The Reign-by-Reign Record of the Rulers of Imperial Rome*. London: Thames & Hudson, 1995. p. 110

p. 50, Shelton, Jo-Ann. *As the Romans Did: A Source Book in Roman Social History*. 2nd ed. New York: Oxford University Press, 1998. p. 292

pp. 50–51, Ibid., p. 292

p. 52, Ibid., pp. 300–301

p. 53, Bartman, Elizabeth. "Hair and the Artifice of Roman Female Adornment." *American Journal of Archaeology* 105, no. 1 (January 2001): p. 4

Chapter 6: Children of the Ruling Class

p. 55, Juvenal. *The Satires*. Translated by G. G. Ramsey. Cambridge, MA: Harvard University Press, 1918. p. 40

p. 56, Shelton, Jo-Ann. *As the Romans Did: A Source Book in Roman Social History*. 2nd ed. New York: Oxford University Press, 1998. p. 32

p. 60, Fantham, Elaine, et al. *Women in the Classical World: Image and Text*. New York: Oxford University Press, 1994. p. 349

Chapter 7: Risk and Rewards

p. 63, Andrews, Robert. *The Columbia Dictionary of Quotations*. New York: Columbia University Press, 1993. p. 191

p. 64, Grabsky, Phil. I, *Caesar: Ruling the Roman Empire*. London: BBC Books, 1997. p. 74

p. 67, *The Historia Augusta*. Lacus Curtius: University of Chicago. Retrieved June 07, 2016. http://penelope.uchicago.edu/Thayer/E/Roman/Texts/Historia_Augusta/home.html.

BIBLIOGRAPHY

Adkins, Lesley, and Roy A. Adkins. *Handbook to Life in Ancient Rome*. New York: Oxford University Press, 1994.

Bartman, Elizabeth. "Hair and the Artifice of Roman Female Adornment." *American Journal of Archaeology* 105, no. 1 (January 2001): 1–25. doi:10.2307/507324.

Boardman, John, et al., eds. *The Oxford Illustrated History of the Roman World*. New York: Oxford University Press, 1988.

Davenport, Basil, eds. *The Portable Roman Reader*. New York: Penguin, 1979.

Editors of Time-Life Books. *Rome: Echoes of Imperial Glory*. Alexandria, VA: Time-Life Books, 1994.

———. *What Life Was Like when Rome Ruled the World: The Roman Empire 100 BC–AD 200*. Alexandria, VA: Time-Life Books, 1997.

Edwards, John. *Roman Cookery: Elegant & Easy Recipes from History's First Gourmet*. rev. ed. Point Roberts, WA: Hartley & Marks, 1986.

Fantham, Elaine, et al. *Women in the Classical World: Image and Text*. New York: Oxford University Press, 1994.

Good, Alexandra. "Knucklebones." Johns Hopkins Archaeological Museum. Retrieved May 02, 2016. http://archaeologicalmuseum.jhu.edu/the-collection/object-stories/archaeology-of-daily-life/childhood/knucklebones.

Grabsky, Phil. I, *Caesar: Ruling the Roman Empire*. London: BBC Books, 1997.

The Historia Augusta. Lacus Curtius: University of Chicago. Retrieved June 07, 2016. http://penelope.uchicago.edu/Thayer/E/Roman/Texts/Historia_Augusta/home.html.

Kamm, Antony. *The Romans: An Introduction*. New York: Routledge, 1995.

Mellor, Ronald, ed. *The Historians of Ancient Rome: An Anthology of the Major Writings*. New York: Routledge, 1998.

Pliny. "To the Emperor Trajan." *Pliny the Younger: Letters*. The Harvard Classics. Retrieved June 07, 2016. http://www.bartleby.com/9/4/2003.

Santosuosso, Antonio. *Storming the Heavens: Soldiers, Emperors, and Civilians in the Roman Empire*. Boulder, CO: Westview Press, 2001.

Scarre, Chris. *Chronicle of the Roman Emperors: The Reign-by-Reign Record of the Rulers of Imperial Rome*. London: Thames & Hudson, 1995.

Shelton, Jo-Ann. *As the Romans Did: A Source Book in Roman Social History*. 2nd ed. New York: Oxford University Press, 1998.

Trentinella, Rosemarie. "Roman Portrait Sculpture: The Stylistic Cycle." *Heilbrunn Timeline of Art History, Metropolitan Museum of Art*. October 2003. http://www.metmuseum.org/toah/hd/ropo2/hd_ropo2.htm.

Wells, Colin. *The Roman Empire*. 2nd ed. Cambridge, MA: Harvard University Press, 1992.

INDEX

Page numbers in **boldface** are illustrations. Entries in **boldface** are glossary terms.